The • Life Cycle • Series

The Life Cycle of a

Sea Horse

Bobbie Kalman

🜊 Crabtree Publishing Company

www.crabtreebooks.com

The Life Cycle Series

A Bobbie Kalman Book

Dedicated by Kristina Lundblad
For Samuel and Philip

Editor-in-Chief
Bobbie Kalman

Writing team
Bobbie Kalman
Kristina Lundblad

Substantive editor
Kathryn Smithyman

Editors
Molly Aloian
Amanda Bishop
Kelley MacAulay
Rebecca Sjonger

Art director
Robert MacGregor

Design
Margaret Amy Reiach

Production coordinator
Heather Fitzpatrick

Photo research
Crystal Foxton

Consultant
Patricia Loesche, Ph.D., Animal Behavior Program,
Department of Psychology, University of Washington

Photographs
Jeffrey Rotman Photography: Jeff Rotman: title page, page 23
© Brandon Cole: page 21 (right)
Seapics.com: © Mark Conlin: pages 15, 16, 19; © Florian Graner: page 21 (left);
    © Mako Hirose: page 28 (bottom); © Rudie Kuiter: pages 13, 17, 18, 25, 27;
    © Gregory Ochocki: page 28 (top); © Doug Perrine: pages 4, 10;
    © Mark Strickland: page 30; © James D. Watt: front cover
Tom Stack & Associates: Dave B. Fleetham: page 3; Gary Milburn: page 29
© Larry Tackett/tackettproductions.com: page 31
Visuals Unlimited: Reinhard Dirscherl: page 20; Bill Kamin: page 24;
    Ken Lucas: pages 5, 22; Marty Snyderman: page 9 (right)
www.norbertwu.com: © 2004 Mark Conlin: page 14; © 2004 Norbert Wu: page 12
Other images by Digital Stock

Illustrations
Barbara Bedell: back cover, series logo, pages 4, 6 (lined sea horse and pygmy
    sea horse), 7 (Pacific sea horse and Australian big-bellied sea horse), 8, 9, 13,
    14, 15, 19, 20, 24, 26, 27, 29, 31
Katherine Kantor: border, pages 7 (short-snouted sea horse), 10, 11, 17, 22, 23
Margaret Amy Reiach: pages 6-7 (background), 18 (right)
Bonna Rouse: page 18 (left)

Crabtree Publishing Company

www.crabtreebooks.com   1-800-387-7650

Cataloging-in-Publication Data
Kalman, Bobbie.
    The life cycle of a sea horse / Bobbie Kalman
        v. cm. -- (The life cycle series)
    Contents: What is a sea horse? -- Spectacular sea horses -- A sea horse's body -
- What is a life cycle? -- Let's dance! -- Growing and hatching -- On their own --
Growing up -- Ready for life -- Forming a bond -- Getting around -- Eating sea
horse style -- Dangers to sea horses -- Helping sea horses.
    ISBN 0-7787-0663-X (RLB) -- ISBN 0-7787-0693-1 (pbk.)
    1. Sea horses--Life cycles--Juvenile literature. [1. Sea horses.] I.Title.
    QL638.S9K35 2004
    597'.6798--dc22
                                                2003027691
                                                CIP

**Published in
the United States**

PMB16A
350 Fifth Ave.
Suite 3308
New York, NY
10118

**Published
in Canada**

616 Welland Ave.
St. Catharines, Ontario
Canada
L2M 5V6

**Published in the
United Kingdom**

White Cross Mills
High Town
Lancaster, LA1 4XS
United Kingdom

**Published
in Australia**

386 Mt. Alexander Rd.
Ascot Vale (Melbourne)
VIC 3032

Contents

What is a sea horse?

Sea horses are fish. Like all fish, sea horses are **cold-blooded** animals. The temperature of their bodies changes with the temperature of the water around them. Fish are also **vertebrate** animals, which means they have backbones. Sea horses have special body parts called **gills** for breathing underwater.

The sea horse's scientific name is "Hippocampus," which comes from the Greek words for "horse" and "sea monster."

Sea horse homes

Sea horses live in oceans all over the world, except the very cold **polar oceans**. They live only in **coastal waters**, or the shallow ocean waters near land. Coastal waters are warm because the sun's rays shine all the way to the ocean floor. Sunlight also helps plants grow there. Sea horses live among plants such as seaweed and sea grass. Coastal waters are also calmer than deep-ocean waters, where **currents** are fast-moving.

Living near reefs

Coral reefs grow on the floor of **tropical oceans**, or the warm oceans near the equator. Coral grows only in coastal waters. Most **species**, or types, of sea horses that live in tropical oceans live near coral reefs.

Four species, including the lined sea horse shown right, live in the coastal waters of the Atlantic Ocean around North America.

Spectacular sea horses

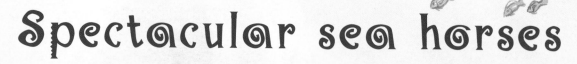

Scientists believe that there are at least 33 different species of sea horses. Some sea horse species are only about one inch (2.5 cm) long, whereas others are much larger. Sea horses are measured from the tops of their heads to the tips of their tails. Males are usually larger than females.

The pygmy sea horse is less than one inch (2.5 cm) long! This species is found in the Pacific Ocean near Australia, southern Japan, Indonesia, and Bali.

The lined sea horse measures about six inches (15 cm) in length. The lined sea horse lives in the Atlantic Ocean, off the coasts of North and South America.

The short-snouted sea horse lives in the Mediterranean Sea and in the Atlantic Ocean off the coasts of European countries. It has a short **snout** and a plump belly. It grows up to five inches (13 cm) long.

The Pacific sea horse is the largest species. It is about fourteen inches (35.5 cm) long! It lives in the waters of the Pacific Ocean, off the coasts of South and North America.

The Australian big-bellied sea horse is the second-largest species, measuring about twelve-and-a-half inches (32 cm) in length. It has a large belly, so sometimes people think the sea horse is carrying babies! It lives in the Pacific Ocean near Australia and New Zealand. This species is also known as the pot-bellied sea horse.

A sea horse's body

A sea horse moves through water by using its fins, but it does not swim the way most fish do. The sea horse travels in an **upright**, or straight up and down, position.

*A sea horse uses its **pectoral fins** to steer.*

*Each sea horse's **coronet**, or "crown," is shaped slightly differently from the coronets of other sea horses of the same species.*

Each of a sea horse's two eyes can look in a different direction.

A sea horse has tiny jaws at the end of its snout.

*The **dorsal fin**, or back fin, is a sea horse's strongest fin. It is used for moving forward through water.*

*A sea horse's **abdomen**, or belly, is the front part of its body. It is located between the head and the base of the tail.*

Taking a breath

A sea horse breathes underwater using gills. Water enters its mouth and flows out through its gills. The gills draw **oxygen** out of the water and send it through the sea horse's body.

*A male sea horse has a **pouch** on its abdomen that is used to hold sea horse eggs. A female sea horse does not have a pouch.*

*A sea horse has a **prehensile tail**, which can curl around and grasp objects such as seaweed.*

Two skeletons

Sea horses belong to a group of fish known as **bony fish**. Like all bony fish, sea horses have skeletons made of bone that support and give shape to their bodies. Each sea horse also has an **external skeleton**.

The tough external skeleton protects the sea horse's body. The external skeleton is made of bony rings, which are **interlocked**, or joined together.

Sea horses have bony plates to protect their bodies, whereas most bony fish are protected by scales.

Sea horse relatives

Sea dragons and pipefish are both related to sea horses. They live in waters near Australia. Pipefish have also been found in other coastal regions—even in regions with fresh water.

Sea dragons look similar to sea horses, but their bodies are longer and more colorful. Sea dragons are also covered in leaflike growths, which make them look like plants.

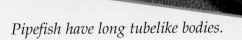

Pipefish have long tubelike bodies.

What is a life cycle?

All animals go through a set of changes called **life cycle**. They are born or **hatch** from eggs. They then **mature**, or become adults. As adults, they are able to make babies of their own. When an animal has a baby, a new life cycle begins.

Life span

A **life span** is not the same as a life cycle. A life span is the length of time an animal is alive. Depending on its species, a sea horse can live from a few months to five years or more. Larger species of sea horses generally live longer than smaller ones do. Scientists do not know exactly how long sea horses live in the **wild** because studying sea horses in the ocean is difficult.

The long-snouted sea horse lives in the Mediterranean Sea and the Atlantic Ocean, off the coasts of Europe.

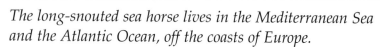

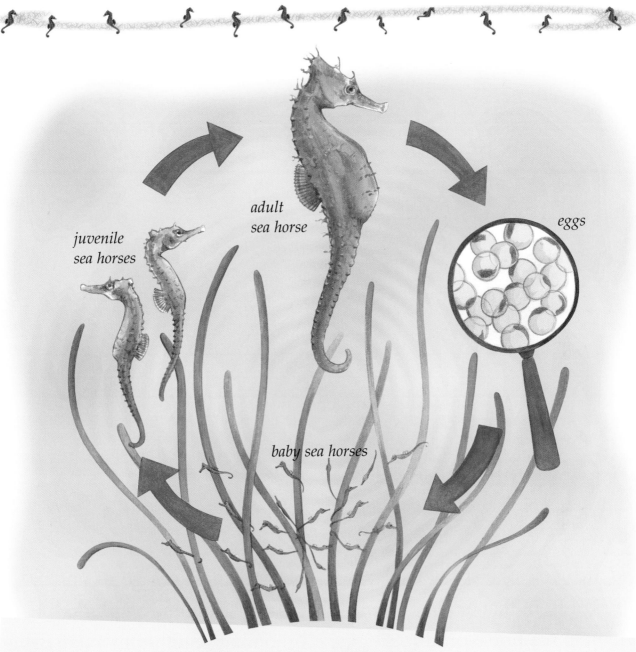

juvenile sea horses

adult sea horse

eggs

baby sea horses

A sea horse's life cycle

Each sea horse begins its life cycle as an **embryo**, or developing baby, inside an egg produced by a female. The eggs are then transferred to a male sea horse's pouch, where the embryos grow. When they hatch, the babies look like tiny adults.

Baby sea horses, called **fry**, live on their own as soon as they leave the pouch. They grow into **juveniles**, or young sea horses that are not yet adults. When they become adults, the sea horses can make babies of their own.

Let's dance!

The life cycle of a sea horse is different from that of most animals. A female sea horse produces eggs, but she does not keep them. Instead, she passes them to her male **mate**, or partner. He then becomes **pregnant** (see page 23). The pregnant male carries the developing embryos inside his body. A male sea horse and a female sea horse begin **mating**, or joining together to make babies, only after they have done a **mating dance**. During the mating dance, they swim together and link their tails, as shown above. A mating dance usually lasts a few minutes, although it may take much longer.

Into the pouch

The mating dance ends when the female passes her eggs to the male. After the last egg is safely inside the male's pouch, the pouch seals up. The male sea horse then stretches and twists his body to settle the eggs comfortably in his pouch. He carries the eggs until the babies hatch and are ready to live in the ocean.

A female sea horse is passing her eggs to her male mate.

male   female

All about eggs

The number of eggs produced by a female sea horse at one time varies depending on the species. Some small sea horse species produce as few as five to ten eggs. Large species can make as many as 1,500 eggs! The females of most species produce 100 to 200 eggs at a time.

Sea horse eggs are so tiny that ten eggs side by side measure only about one inch (2.5 cm)!

Growing and hatching

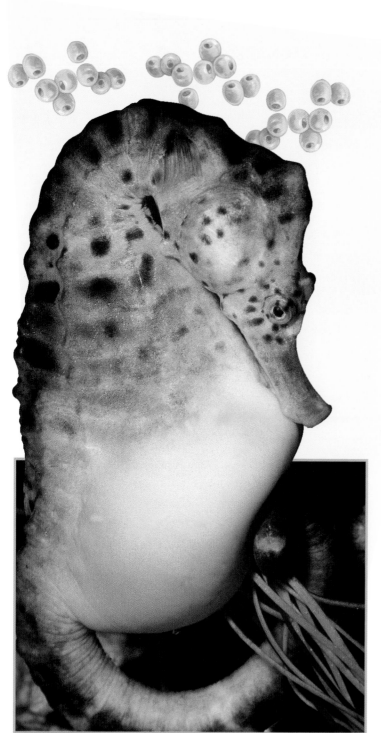

A male sea horse is pregnant for two to four weeks. The length of a pregnancy depends on the sea horse's species and on the temperature of the water in which it lives. Species that live in very warm waters have shorter pregnancies than species that live in cold waters.

A good place to grow

The **lining**, or walls, of the pouch form a pocket around each egg. The lining carries oxygen from the father's body to the embryos. Each egg also holds a **yolk**. The yolk provides **nutrients**, or food energy, for the developing embryos.

The father's body protects the embryos so well that almost every embryo hatches.

Too big to move

Each sea horse embryo develops and grows inside its egg. As the embryos get larger, the father's pouch stretches to make room. Near the end of his pregnancy, a male sea horse rarely moves. He often curls his tail around some seaweed and remains completely still for several days!

Breaking out

When the embryos are fully formed, they hatch from their eggs. They do not leave the pouch immediately, however. They remain in the pouch and feed on leftover bits of yolk. When the food is gone, the babies swim out of the pouch.

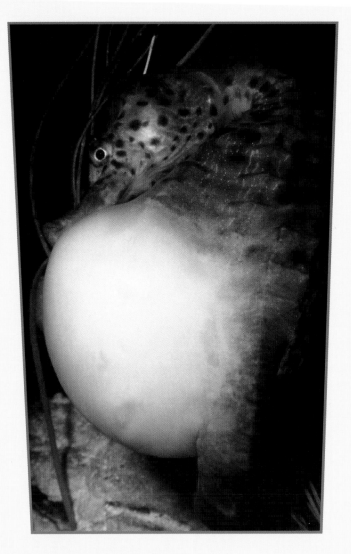

A little at a time

Ocean water is salty. The father's pouch contains liquid that becomes salty during his pregnancy. By the time the embryos hatch, the liquid is as salty as ocean water. Living in this liquid allows the baby sea horses to get used to living in salt water, so they will not get a shock when they swim out of the pouch into the ocean.

Out of the pouch

A male sea horse senses when it is time for the babies to leave the pouch. Males usually release their babies at night. It can take several hours, or even several days, for all the babies to swim out of the pouch. They swim out a few at a time. If the male is having a difficult time getting the babies to swim out of the pouch, he may rub his pouch on something hard, such as some coral or a rock, as shown above. Rubbing against a hard surface pushes the babies out.

Goodbye, Dad!

When the baby sea horses swim out of the pouch, they are tiny. Most are about half an inch (7-12 mm) long, depending on the species. Despite their small sizes, the babies must survive on their own and find food without help from either of their parents.

Look closely

Baby sea horses may look like miniature adults, but they are still growing. Their bony plates are not yet hard. The babies do have some protection, however. They are nearly **transparent**, or "see through." Lack of color makes them difficult to see in the water, which helps protect them from **predators**, or animals that catch and eat other animals.

No matter how brightly colored a male sea horse normally is, he grows pale and gray while he is releasing the babies.

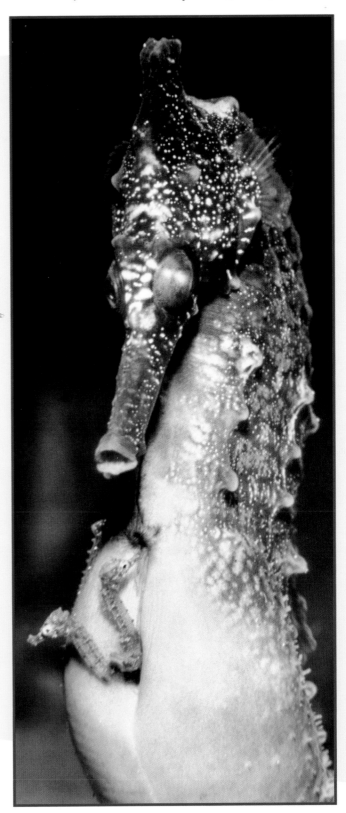

On their own

Baby sea horses grow quickly during the first two months of their lives. They feed continuously on tiny ocean creatures, such as baby shrimp, worms, and insects.

A dangerous time

Sea horse babies are well protected in the pouch, but they face many dangers as soon as they swim out into the ocean. Predators such as fish, penguins, crabs, sea turtles, and larger sea horses catch and eat baby and juvenile sea horses. In fact, only five out of every 1,000 young sea horses survive!

When baby sea horses leave the pouch, they do not swim upright as adults do. For their first few days outside the pouch, they swim headfirst through the water.

Colorful juveniles

When a juvenile is a few weeks old, color starts to appear on its external skeleton. Color first appears on the juvenile's head and tail. It then spreads across the entire body. Gradually, the young sea horse develops the stripes and spots that are common to its species. It takes up to one year for a juvenile to become a fully grown adult.

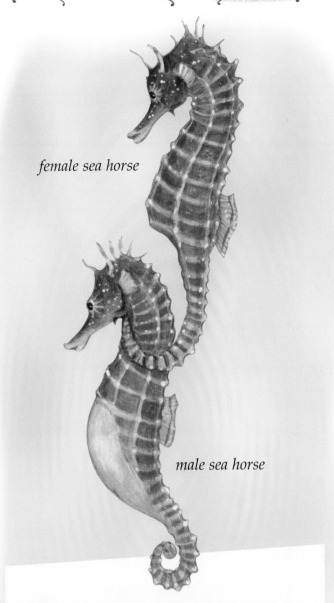

female sea horse

male sea horse

As a young sea horse grows, its snout gets longer.

The proof is in the pouch

Scientists cannot tell if a sea horse is male or female until it is between four and eight months old. At this age, a juvenile male's pouch becomes visible. Some male juveniles also develop color patches where their pouches are located. Juveniles without pouches are female.

All grown up

By the time a sea horse is mature, its body has **adapted**, or changed to help it survive. Its external skeleton is now completely hard. In some species, the external skeleton is also covered by many **cirri**, which are tough spines that help protect a sea horse from predators. Predators eat fewer adult sea horses than babies because the adults are so prickly!

How they change color

An adult sea horse's skin has tiny cells, called **chromatophores**, which are filled with colored chemicals. The sea horse's brain sends messages to these cells, causing one or more of them to open or close. When the sea horse is hiding in green seaweed, it can become dark green. If the sea horse moves near orange coral, however, the chromatophores that control orange open and the sea horse's body blends in with the orange coral.

Blending in

Camouflage is coloring or patterning on an animal's body that allows it to blend in with its surroundings. Camouflage helps adult sea horses stay safe. To blend in, adult sea horses change the shade of their skins. The shape of their cirri also helps them hide. The cirri look like coral, sea grass, or other plants among which sea horses live.

All alone

Adult sea horses live on their own, rather than in groups. If they lived in groups, they would attract the attention of predators. A sea horse that is on its own is difficult for predators to spot regardless of its surroundings.

A sea horse sometimes wraps its tail around itself and rolls into a ball to hide from predators.

The spines on this sea horse's head and back are cirri. They help the sea horse hide among rocks and sea grasses.

Forming a bond

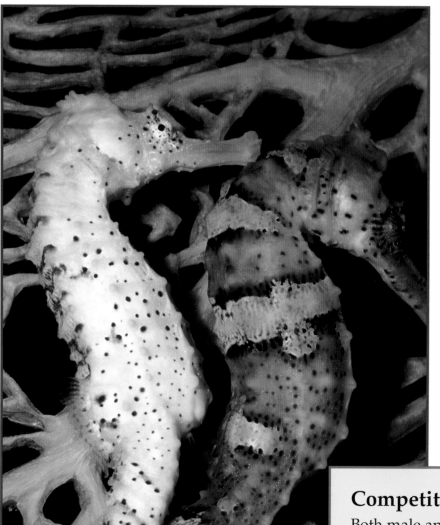

Although mature sea horses live alone, males eventually seek out female mates. The male shows interest in making babies by beginning a mating dance. If the female takes part in the dance, they form a **pair bond**, or a mating partnership.

Competition for females

Both male and female sea horses compete for mates, but the males are more aggressive in their competitions. Scientists have observed males wrestling one another with their tails and nipping each other's fins to win over a female.

Loyal bonds

Once a male and a female sea horse dance together, they will make babies only with each other. This type of relationship is called **monogamous**. A pair bond stays in contact during the male's pregnancy by dancing for several minutes each day. A male sea horse will only seek out a new partner if its mate dies or grows too old to produce eggs.

Giving away her eggs

A mature female sea horse has eggs in her body. When the mating dance is finished, she transfers her eggs to her partner through a long, thin tube called an **ovipositor**. The female sends her eggs through this tube into the male's pouch. When the eggs are inside his pouch, the male **fertilizes** them by adding a liquid from his body called **sperm**. Baby sea horses grow only from fertilized eggs.

After releasing the babies from his pouch, a male sea horse is soon ready for another mating dance—often that same day!

Getting around

Sea horses are not fast swimmers. Being slow can help them, however! Rapid movements might attract unwanted attention from predators. Slow-moving sea horses stay mainly in one place. Sometimes sea horses do not move at all—they wrap their tails around plants and "float" in the water. By hanging on, sea horses are less likely to be noticed by predators. Holding on to plants also helps prevent sea horses from being swept away in strong currents.

Different sea horse species rarely meet one another. Each species lives in its own area of the ocean.

The swim bladder

Although sea horses are slow, they have a lot of control over their movements. They move forward and steer using their fins. Sea horses also move up and down in the water by using an organ called

a **swim bladder**. The swim bladder is like a bag of air. To move upward in water, the sea horse draws air into its swim bladder. To move downward, the sea horse lets out some of the air.

A sea horse's largest and strongest fin is its dorsal fin. The dorsal fin can move back and forth as many as 35 times per second!

Eating sea-horse style

Sea horses eat a lot of food. Ocean water contains tiny animals that sea horses catch and eat. One sea horse can eat up to 3,000 **brine shrimp** a day!

*When **prey**, or an animal that can be eaten, floats by, the sea horse stretches out its neck and quickly sucks it up with its snout.*

Be patient!

Since a sea horse generally stays in one place anchored by its tail, it cannot roam the ocean floor looking for food. Each of its two eyes can see in a different direction. A sea horse can search for prey with one eye and look out for predators with the other eye—at the same time!

A "built-in straw"

A sea horse sucks food through its tubelike snout. The snout works in the same way as a drinking straw does. The sea horse uses it to suck food into its mouth quickly. Sea horses do not have teeth, so they cannot bite or chew their food. They feed only on animals that are small enough to fit through their tiny jaws.

Eating all the time

A sea horse does not have a stomach for storing food. Since it cannot store food, it must eat constantly to survive. It may eat for as many as ten hours a day!

Dangers to sea horses

Sea horses are amazing animals! Unfortunately, some species are in trouble in some areas. The Krysna sea horse, shown above, is **endangered**, or at risk of dying out in the natural places where it lives. Like all sea horses, its greatest threat is the dangerous actions of people.

Overfishing has greatly reduced the number of sea horses living in oceans. This threat is especially a problem off the coasts of Asia, where sea horses are caught and dried. Some are sold to tourists as souvenirs, but many more are ground up and used in medicines.

海　馬
10g 3500円

Harming their homes

People also harm sea horses by **polluting** the oceans. Pollution from ships, oil spills, and **sewage** poisons oceans. It kills some animals and makes others sick. Coral reefs are made up of living animals, and pollution kills large areas of these reefs. When coral reefs die, sea horses have fewer places to live. Big ships also create waves underwater as they pass, damaging the grassy areas where sea horses live. If these threats are not reduced, sea horses may become **extinct**, or disappear from the Earth forever.

Sea horses in aquariums

Sea horses are so beautiful that many people buy them as pets. They are very sensitive animals, however, and usually survive less than one year in aquariums. Sea horses must always be in an environment where there are many tiny animals available for them to eat. Most **captive** sea horses, or those in aquariums, starve to death! Captive sea horses also rarely have babies—they do not complete their life cycles.

You can help sea horses and other animals living in oceans by taking care of the environment. If you live near an ocean, ask an adult to help you find out about or organize a shore cleanup.

Harmful chemicals

Sea horses and other fish cannot live in water that is polluted. Chemicals that are sprayed on fields and lawns wash into the oceans, making them unhealthy places for animals. Ask your parents and neighbors to use **organic**, or natural, sprays that do not damage oceans. Also, switch to **biodegradable** soaps and detergents so that fewer chemicals will go down drains and end up in oceans.

The tiger tail sea horse is yellow and black in color, with stripes along its body. This species lives in the waters near Asia, where sea horse fishing is popular.

Sea horse research

Many people are working to find out more about sea horses. **Project Seahorse** is a group of scientists who study sea horses all over the world. They are working to protect the areas where sea horses live. Another goal of the project is to spread awareness about the dangers of overfishing sea horses and selling them to make souvenirs and medicines.

Start surfing!

A great way to help sea horses is to learn more about them. Check out the following websites:

- *www.pbs.org/wgbh/nova/seahorse*
- *www.projectseahorse.org*

Another discovery!

A new species of sea horse was discovered off the coast of Indonesia in May 2003 by a Project Seahorse scientist. It is named *Hippocampus denise*, after photographer Denise Tackett. The new species is the smallest sea horse—an adult is just over half an inch (1.3 cm) long! This tiny sea horse lives among corals.

The new species, shown left, is attached by its tail to a sea fan.

Glossary

Note: Boldfaced words that are defined in the book may not appear in the glossary.

biodegradable Describing a substance that can be broken down naturally by bacteria in the environment

brine shrimp A tiny species of shrimp

captive Describing an animal living in a zoo or aquarium; not in the wild

coral reef An area of the ocean made up of living coral and coral skeletons

current A flow of water that moves continuously in a certain direction

fertilize To add sperm to an egg so a baby can form

hatch To break out of an egg

mate (n) A mating partner; (v) To join together to make babies

overfishing To take too many of one species of fish from an area of the ocean

oxygen A gas in the air that humans and animals need to breathe

polar oceans The oceans around the North or the South Poles that have frigid temperatures

pollute To add waste or chemicals that harm living things to air, water, or soil

sewage Waste that is carried from sinks, toilets, and other drains

snout The front part of an animal's head, including the nose, mouth, and jaws

sperm A male reproductive cell that joins with a female's egg to make babies

wild A place not controlled by people, where plants and animals live naturally

Index

3 4 5 6 7 8 9 0 Printed in the U.S.A. 3 2 1 0 9 8 7 6